Whales

by Grace Hansen

ABDO
OCEAN LIFE
Kids

abdopublishing.com

Published by Abdo Kids, a division of ABDO, PO Box 398166, Minneapolis, Minnesota 55439.

Copyright © 2015 by Abdo Consulting Group, Inc. International copyrights reserved in all countries. No part of this book may be reproduced in any form without written permission from the publisher.

Printed in the United States of America, North Mankato, Minnesota.

102014

012015

 THIS BOOK CONTAINS RECYCLED MATERIALS

Photo Credits: iStock, Seapics.com, Shutterstock, Thinkstock, © Gabriel Barathieu / CC-BY-SA-2.0 p15

Production Contributors: Teddy Borth, Jennie Forsberg, Grace Hansen

Design Contributors: Laura Rask, Dorothy Toth

Library of Congress Control Number: 2014943669

Cataloging-in-Publication Data

Hansen, Grace.

Whales / Grace Hansen.

p. cm. -- (Ocean life)

ISBN 978-1-62970-713-6 (lib. bdg.)

Includes index.

1. Whales--Juvenile literature.   I. Title.

599.5--dc23

2014943669

Table of Contents

Whales

Whales live in oceans around the world.

There are two types of
whales. There are baleen
and toothed whales.
All whales are **mammals**.

Baleen Whales

Baleen whales are very large. They **filter** feed. They mainly eat **plankton**.

8

A blue whale is a baleen whale. It is the largest **mammal** to ever live.

Toothed Whales

Toothed whales have teeth. They eat fish, squid, and much more.

12

A sperm whale is a toothed whale. It has a giant head. Its brain is larger than any other animal's.

Body Parts

All whales have **flippers** and **flukes**. These help them move in the water. Most whales have a **dorsal fin**.

16

dorsal fin

fluke

flipper

17

All whales breathe through blowholes. Baleen whales have two blowholes. Toothed whales have one.

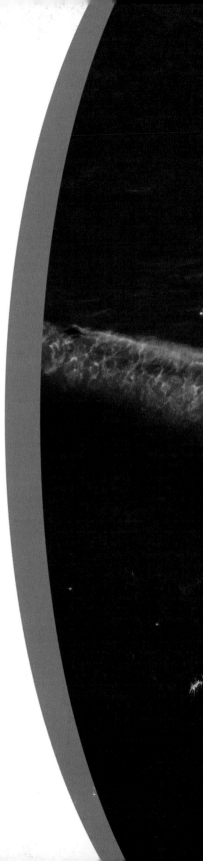

blowhole

19

Migration

Many whales travel very far. They move from cold to warmer waters. Whales find food in colder waters. Whales have babies in warmer waters.

More Facts

- Beluga whales are also called white whales. They are one of the few whales that do not have a **dorsal fin**. They live up to 50 years in the wild.

- Humpback whales are known for the sounds they make. The sounds they make can go on for hours. They are very complex. Scientists believe they are talking to other humpbacks.

- Sperm whales are easily spotted by the shape of their heads. Their large heads most likely help them with deep diving.

Glossary

dorsal fin – a fin that is found on most whales' backs.

filter – remove food from water.

flipper – a large flat limb used for swimming.

fluke – one of the lobes of a whale's tail.

mammal – a warm-blooded animal that has hair and whose females produce milk to feed their young.

plankton – very small animals that drift through the ocean. Many large ocean animals eat them.

Index

abdokids.com

Use this code to log on to abdokids.com and access crafts, games, videos, and more!

Abdo Kids Code:
OWK7136